EVERYBODY
A LITTLE

T L C

TRANSFORMATIONAL   LIFESTYLE   CONTENT

90 DAYS

OF SELF-AWARENESS, SELF-ESTEEM,
SELF-CONFIDENCE, AND SELF-WORTH

PRESENTED BY

TAWAWN LOWE

TLC
PUBLISHING COMPANY

www.tawawn.com

EVERYBODY NEEDS A LITTLE **TLC**

Transformational Lifestyle Content

90 Days of Self-Awareness, Self-Esteem, Self-Confidence, and Self-Worth

Library of Congress Cataloging-in-Publication Data is available upon request.

ISBN: 978-0-9788090-8-9

E-Book ISBN: 978-1-64786-076-9

DISCLAIMER

Although you may find the affirmative expressions to be useful, the book is sold with the understanding that neither the co-authors nor TLC Publishing Company, are engaged in presenting any legal, relationship, financial, emotional, or health advice. The purpose of this book is to educate and entertain. The co-authors and publishers shall neither assume liability nor responsibility for anyone with respect to any loss or damage caused directly or indirectly by the information in the book.

Any person who is experiencing financial, anxiety, depression, health, mental health, or relationship issues should consult with a licensed therapist, advisor, licensed psychologist, or other qualified professional before commencing into anything described in this book. This book intends to provide you with the writers' insights and reflections on the four subjects in the book. All results will differ; however, our goal is to provide you with affirmative expressions to use as a practical approach to foster powerful change within your life.

EVERYBODY NEEDS A LITTLE **TLC**

Transformational Lifestyle Content

90 Days of Self-Awareness, Self-Esteem, Self-Confidence and Self-Worth

TO: _____

FROM: _____

This book is dedicated to my biggest cheerleader who's always praying, encouraging, and supporting with being the person created to be, my mother Charlotte Harrison. I want to thank you for always pushing, believing and praying for me. I'm glad God choose you to be my mother.

I LOVE YOU!

This book is also dedicated to those who are not, or working on becoming more self-aware, struggling with their self-esteem, self-confidence and self-worth; those who know they need to start healing, so they can start living.

We want you to know that you are not alone on your journey, and that you have the power to learn, grow, and become your best self. All you need is

A Little TLC!

TABLE OF CONTENTS

SELF-ESTEEM & SELF-CONFIDENCE 57

SELF-WORTH 95

Acknowledgments

SEVERAL PEOPLE HAVE contributed in various ways to the completion and success of this book, and we are most grateful for their efforts. First, TLC Publishing Company would like to acknowledge the nineteen collaborative authors who took this journey with us. It is through their powerful expressions that we will strive to provide insight, change minds, and offer new perspectives to the readers who are challenged, or need encouragement and understanding about self-awareness, self-esteem, self-confidence, and self-worth.

I want to thank them all for their boldness and bravery to let their voices be heard so that others can be healed. Each author has shared a personal part of themselves, their experiences, and lessons learned through their written expressions.

THANK YOU FOR YOUR SUPPORT!!

Rev. Dawn W. Adams	Rev. Dr. Tikeisha Harris
Sandy Buchan-Sumter	Tasha Graham
Dr, Salim Bilal-Edwards	Candice Jackson
Pamishia Boyd	Dr. Rasheda Parks
Angela Jewel Brown	Nanyamka Payne
Yolanda 'Loni' Chinn	Kim Reed-Butler
Gail Crowder	Trgina Renae Hunter

Morgan Chapman   Rev. Sandra Williams

Tarnisha Esco   Sonya Webb

Dr. Sharon Foreman

We also want to acknowledge and thank all the those behind the scene, who have supported this project through services or prayers. A special shout out goes to Pen Legacy® (Charron Monaye) for their coaching and mentorship, Next Leveling Publishing for capturing our vision for the Series book cover designs, Nicole Kennedy Green for editing, Junnita Jackson for the book layout, Anita's Designs (Anita Gillspie) for designing all our promotional materials, and Concierges Elite (Taniesha Williams) for their virtual assistant services that kept me on track in every phase of this project.

The success of TLC Publishing Company on this project is in part due to many who have encouraged and prayed for me and have worked tirelessly to get us across the finish line. My heart is grateful, and I love and appreciate you all.

Introduction

THE EVERYBODY NEEDS A Little TLC Series books are a collection of transformational lifestyle content in the form of affirmative expressions that focus on personal development topics that contributes to intentional, mindful and purposeful living. The first Series of the collection is 90-Days of Self-Awareness, Self-Esteem, Self-Confidence, and Self-Worth.

We believe everybody needs a little TLC! No, we are not talking about tender loving care, but transformational lifestyle content (TLC). The TLC needed to encourage and equip you in your continuous mission of becoming the best version of yourselves, and creating the happiness and success you desire. A big part of being intentional, becoming your best self, and achieving your desires requires you to make a simple, yet hard decisions. You must make a decision about who you want to be, how you want to show up, and what you want for your life. How you answer these questions is based on your understanding of yourself, life lessons and experiences, your beliefs, feelings and thoughts, and how you value yourself. All these elements are intertwined, and play a vital role in how you navigate and progress in your journey.

Through my own life journey, I have learned that we create our lives with beliefs, thoughts, and actions, and let's not forget, with our words. As a coach, mentor and trainer, over the last seven years, I have interacted with thousands of people from individual clients, and people from organizations of all sizes nationwide. They all want to know how to make profound and sustainable change, change behaviors, and become more result oriented. They are looking for that secret formula, or what some call the secret sauce that brings forth viable transformation. In my study of myself, people, my education and credentials, and work with people, I have determined there are four elements of change that are interconnected. These four elements prevent people from fully maximizing their potential, but can also bring forth massive transformation in your life. Self-awareness, self-esteem, self-confidence, and self-worth have a great impact on your outlook and belief about oneself, how you show up in the world, and the sum of success you achieve. When you do not have a good handle on who you are, what makes you tick, why you tick the way you do, or understand the importance of your being and worth, it's impossible for you to take full charge of your life, happiness, or success. The truth is life has life us all, and our experiences have sometimes made us strong, and on some occasions caused us to relinquish our power to be, do, and become. We all at some point and time have been influenced by our life experiences. To the point where we no longer believed in ourselves, thought we were good enough, believed we didn't deserve happiness, or, if our life had any meaning. The beauty is, you, me, we all have the ability to reclaim our power. When you are walking in your power, you can change what you believe and think about yourselves, the world, and the direction you take your life. Regaining your power starts with taking full responsibility for your lives. To take 100% responsibility for your life means, you take responsibility for your beliefs, thoughts, and actions.

Now I know it sounds cliché, but everything you need to take responsibility is within you. It really does start with self-exploration and having wisdom and insight into yourself. When you are willing to face yourself, start asking those hard questions, and getting to the root of your actions, beliefs, thoughts and words; you can start shifting your focus, and the vibration of your energy. Change requires the willingness to be open, trusting of the process, think and speak positive, and abandon your fixed mindset for a growth mindset. Self-awareness, self-esteem, self-confidence and self-worth are the core to what makes us who we are. When you take charge of your life, you take charge of what you believe, feel, think, and know about yourself. If you are ready to refine these core areas of your being, it's time to give yourself a little TLC!

Everybody Needs A Little TLC Series was created to provide the reader with just the right amount of TLC to support them on their journey of taking charge of their lives, destiny, practicing self-love/self-care, exploring what they want, to dream big, become goal-oriented, and to reach that next level of emotional, personal and professional wellness and success. The visionary of the Series was intentional with focusing the first book on the four core elements that play an integral role in transformation. She believes using affirmative expressions to focus on these four core elements is a simple approach to influence your thoughts, and initiate a powerful change. The visionary and collaborative authors in this book did not write their expressions as people who have always been self-assured, never lacking low self-esteem, confidence, or self-worth, but individuals who took charge of their life. What they all have in common is that they prevailed in regaining their power, and are in charge of their lives and destiny; and they want that for you.

Who is this book for?

Believe it or not, this book is created for everybody. Everybody who understands the importance of self-awareness, self-esteem, self-confidence and self-worth. This book is a reminder for those individuals who have already made themselves a priority, practicing emotional and physical wellness, and are in tune with their feelings. The reminder is to stay the course, because you are doing it.

This book is also for those individuals who have yet to discover who they are, what they can become, or achieve, and are wandering through life, waiting for life to happen. It is for those who are stuck, feeling discouraged, and need that push to take back their power. It also for those who have started their journey of self-discovery and still need encouragement and inspiration because there will be days when they will need a little TLC!

The goal of this book is to use affirmative expressions to help feed your mind positive thoughts, to shift your perspective where needed, and provide a method to help you foster the changes you want to see. In 90-days you have the ability to change your attitude, perspective and direction of your life. Are you ready?

How do you use this book?

The book consists of 90 days of affirmative expressions and declarations that require a consistent ritual to take action to positively feed your mind. For 90 days, we challenge you to take the following steps:

1. Read and reflect on one affirmative expression more than one time a day.
2. Say the declaration to yourself, then say it to yourself aloud.
3. Don't force yourself to believe, just say it, repeat it several times.
4. Write down what resonated with you, journaling your feeling and thoughts and what the words mean to you.
5. Be open and allow the expressions to boost your mind power.

Remember, we create our lives with our feelings, thoughts and actions. Let your emotionally wellness be one of your biggest goals – because you need it to be in charge of your life and destiny. Everything you need is within; you have the ability to reclaim your power.

Are you ready?

It's time, time to give yourself a little TLC!

Tawawn Lowe

Self-Awareness

"The person in life that you will always be with the most is yourself. Because even when you are with others, you are still with yourself, too! When you wake up in the morning, you are with yourself, lying in bed at night, you are with yourself, walking down the street in the sunlight you are with yourself. What kind of person do you want to walk with down the street? What kind of person do you want to wake with in the morning? What kind of person do you want to see at the end of the day before you fall asleep? The person you will be with is yourself, and it's your responsibility to be that person you want to be. I know I want to spend my life with a person who knows how to let things go, is not full of hate, who can smile and be carefree. So that's who I have to be."

– C. JoyBell C.

Self-Awareness

The conscious knowledge of one's own character, feelings, motives, and desires.
An awareness of one's own personality or individuality.

Beloved,

This gift called life is a journey with many destinations. As you continue to embark upon your life journey, my prayer is that your life will be enlightened through a state of becoming self-aware. Getting to know thy self is one of the greatest gifts you can give to yourself. It is a conscious decision. An awakening to self that leads to a journey of self-exploration and self-investigation. A process to go inward, to take an honest look at yourself, and examine your behavior, feelings, and thinking. Self-awareness is necessary for real change, growth, healing, and transformation to take place.

It is your "**YES**" to expand your ability to have a deeper understanding of yourself.

To lack self-awareness is disempowering. It limits your ability to maximize your potential, find your purpose, be in full control of your destiny, and achieve the happiness and success you desire. Becoming self-aware is a gift that provides you the opportunity to release yourself from the emotional and mental bondage that keeps you from becoming your best self, creating your best life, and living life on your terms.

Everybody Needs A Little TLC!

Self-awareness is empowering. It is the TLC you need to be in harmony, and know who you are.

DAY 1

To Know Thy Self

TO KNOW THY self is to become intimately acquainted with oneself. Your relationship with yourself is vital to your overall well-being and success. Getting in touch with you, and being self-aware is a part of your journey in becoming the best version of yourself. It is the greatest gift you can give yourself. It is your YES, to an intimate connection that gives you the ability to reflect, think, and learn what you like, you don't like, and what you want or don't want for your life. Getting to know yourself allows you to get more intimate with your fears, feelings, flaws, thoughts, motivation, and strengths, which impacts your happiness, joy, peace, and success.

To know thy self is like being a master in the game of chess. A master of chess understands the importance of insight and how it impacts what moves to make. When you truly know yourself, you have insight that allows you to be more calculating and intentional about the moves you need to make for the impact you desire. To know yourself is to become a master of yourself.

Declaration: TODAY I start the journey of becoming the master of myself. I will take some quiet time each day to get better acquainted with myself so that I can be calculating in my moves to better myself and my life.

Tawawn Lowe

DAY 2

It's An "Inside Out" Day

IT'S EASY TO stay true to yourself when you know who you are. When you don't know who you are, begin by looking inward. You'll find yourself from the inside out. What you see outside may not reflect what's inside. Don't let a mirror be your judge, and don't just take a peek at your true feelings, motives, and desires. Spend some quality time to look deep within and own your thoughts, acknowledge your strengths, and accept your shortcomings. We all have something to feel good about; none of us is perfect.

Your inner spirit desires to be seen. Show yourself so you can see yourself, and be free in who you were created to be.

Declaration: TODAY I will be seen from the "Inside Out".

Rev. Sandra Williams

DAY 3

Knowing Yourself is Knowing that You Have a Destiny

KNOWING YOURSELF IS knowing you have a destiny to fulfill, and it depends on the choices *you* make. Your life's journey is contingent on what dreams and aspirations you have, the morals and values you practice, and how you align them to direct your life's path. Allowing anything or anyone to sojourn your goals or change your moral compass is an absolute detour from your destiny. It will only guide you in the direction of disappointment and self-pity. You must love yourself enough to accept responsibility for your decisions, actions, and reactions above all else. Knowing yourself and staying true to who you are will make your journey a smooth ride.

Declaration: TODAY I will focus on my goals and refuse to allow anything to block me in the process – I know myself, love myself, and will never change myself for anyone but me!

Dr. Rasheda Parks

DAY 4

Seek, and You Shall Find

"**THE ROAD OF** life can only reveal itself as it is traveled; each turn in the road reveals a surprise. Man's future is hidden."

<u>Declaration</u>: TODAY I will be open and allow my journey to reveal the future I want for myself.

Author Unknown

DAY 5

Your Journey belongs to you!

SELF-AWARENESS BEGINS WITH acknowledging that your journey belongs to you and you alone. On this journey, you have the power to start, to pause, to stop, and to start again. You are not on anyone else's schedule. We all do ourselves a disservice by trying to adhere to the timeframes and constraints that society has placed in the atmosphere. How about adapting to the notion that you're finished when it's finished, whatever the "it", is. We all tend to overthink, over-analyze, and overcompensate for the things that we think we lack. We spend a lot of time on the what-ifs, and the 'I should haves' and the maybes. Let's refocus on the great things we have accomplished!! The small goals we've set for ourselves. This journey will require you to change your mind often, change your strategy, and even change the company you keep.

You may very well find yourself trekking alone, and your Self-esteem will **PUSH** you to your intended end. **I implore you to get a song and put it deep in your heart, learn this song.** Make sure that the lyrics speak to you and speaks to your soul. Now journey on!

<u>Declaration</u>: TODAY I will RECALL the steps that I have taken to get me here!

Sonya D. Webb

DAY 6

You Are You

THE BEST GIFT you can give yourself is loving YOU, flaws and all. Treating yourself to dinner and a movie and enjoying your company is a sign of being comfortable with who you are. You are a work in progress, being fully aware that you have worked out those kinks that were stumbling blocks in your past.

No one knows you better than you, for you are an overcomer and your own best cheerleader. You are YOU!!

<u>Declaration</u>: TODAY I love myself because God loves me. I am fearfully and wonderfully made. I am special in God's eyes; therefore, I am special! I am uniquely ME, and I fully embrace ALL OF ME!

Kim Reed-Butler

DAY 7

Freedom to Be Starts with You

IT'S TIME TO take your first step to freedom. To maximize your abilities, you must first know yourself. Other people can tell you who they think you are, but you know yourself better than anyone else. You only need to look within. Get ready to expand your influence and enhance your productivity. You will have to admit your strengths, access your weakness, and face your fears. Refuse to wear the mask of other people's perceptions of you. This process will stretch your beliefs and awaken your trues desires.

For success in life, there is no one-size-fits-all package. The fact that you don't seem to fit in somewhere does not mean you are insignificant everywhere. So, take that step! Look into your soul and find the giant that lives within.

Declaration: TODAY I choose to access myself and accept my discoveries. I refuse to wear the mask of what others think, or what is not true about me.

Pamishia Boyd

DAY 8

You Know You

YOU KNOW YOU. You know who you are, including your flaws and strengths. You are focused and strong. Knowing who you are is a strength that will propel you to greater heights. Once you recognize who you are, the world can't restrain you from living out your potential.

<u>Declaration</u>: TODAY I am aware of who I was, who I am now, and the person I have the potential to be. I am comfortable in my skin.

Angela Jewel Brown

DAY 9

I am Important Too Me

IF YOU DON'T know who you are or why you do the things you do, it's time you figure that out. It can feel overwhelming even to begin this journey. It's 100% worth it. The beginning is the first step to living your best life. You will figure out what to keep and what to discard. You may get push back from certain people in your life because they are used to you being a certain way. But you being happy with who you are **is also** important.

I started my journey years ago. It's almost a never-ending one because I'm changing every year I get older. I've had great support, but I've also had opposition. I kept going. I did become aware of who I truly am and what I've been hiding. I'm so much happier with myself, and people can see that as well.

Be courageous to start your journey. I encourage you to begin your journey of self-awareness. The piece of mind you will have as you start to accept every aspect of who you are is priceless. When distractions come your way- and they will- remind yourself that you are important too. When emotions are high as you find out what you've been hiding from yourself, keep going. No matter how long it takes, prioritize your journey.

<u>Declaration</u>: TODAY I will spend all the time I need on myself. I am important too.

Candice Jackson

DAY 10

Seek to Learn – Learn and Take Action

"**TO LOOK IS** one thing, to see what you look at is another, to understand what you see is a third, to learn from what you understand is still something else, but to act on what you learn is all that really matters! How do I act?"

Declaration: TODAY I will use each day to take action from the lessons I am learning from my journey of self-discovery.

Author Unknown

DAY 11

Authentically You

TAKE THE TIME to know yourself and the abilities that you possess. Don't let anyone or anything define who you should be. People love labels and titles to identify who we are or the need to being a part of a clique to make us feel special or worthy. But who are you? It's so simple! You are the human race. Part of a people living in this world, walking in purpose because of chaos in this world. Whatever your status, income, or profession, you should never be too big of a person not to help someone else who is hurting from the weight of life. When you are confident in who you are, you can extend a hand to give help, pray, encourage, and hold in high-esteem another individual knowing that God only made one authentic you.

When you can authentically be you, not the person on the right of you, or the one standing behind you, there should be no room for envy or jealousy. When you know that you are authentically you inside and all of that Godly fabulousness shows on the outside, there is no hesitation to be yourself. It doesn't matter if you are plain and simple or flamboyant and fabulous the significant thing is to know who you are. The flipside of that is the knowledge that you are authentic in who you are becoming even in growth.

There is something on the inside that makes you unique. You are the brand ambassador of yourself. Queen wear your crown. Know and understand that we each have a purpose and a great gift. Only you can reveal your gift to the world so that it may change the environment or alter the atmosphere, and that gift is being authentically you.

Declaration: TODAY is the day to be the best authentic you!

Tasha Graham

DAY 12

Knowing Yourself

KNOWING YOURSELF IS the beginning of your journey to doing what you were created to do. Identifying, acknowledging, and using your gifts and talents to touch the lives of others are key to knowing who you are. Recognizing what inspires or motivates you and operating on those incentives will lead you to your purpose and, ultimately, your destiny. Pouring your life's energy into a purpose that's fulfilling and satisfying to your inner spirit and also blesses those you serve, confirms that you know who you are.

Don't get caught up in the "how" and "when," just stay ready to walk in your purpose as life unfolds and opportunities are presented. You'll recognize yourself when you begin to be yourself. Your inner spirit will awaken to all that you are meant to be.

Declaration: TODAY I know who I am. I know myself!

Rev. Sandra Williams

DAY 13

Dig Deep

WHAT MAKES YOU smile? What angers you? How do you respond to fear? The answers you provide to these questions are insights into who you are and how you react to things. Knowing yourself is one of the most valuable insights that you can have in your life. However, many people don't seem to be self-aware.

Understanding yourself is not just about being able to say, "This is who I am." It allows you to recognize why you may be getting stuck in ruts that won't allow you to actualize the life you want. Digging deeper into why you respond or don't respond to certain situations are indicators of your motivators. Behind actions and inactions are more in-depth stories of your life. Perhaps you become triggered by loud voices, causing you not to speak up. If you fail to realize that aspect of yourself, you will always stay quiet when others exhibit that behavior. However, once you have made that connection, you can adjust. Rather than shrinking back, you could address their tone. Perhaps, now your response will be to take a deep breath and remind yourself you are in a safe space you don't have to hide.

Learn yourself. Know yourself. It may help unlock the areas where you've been stuck. Maybe the reason you haven't found love, or gotten the promotion, or started your business is that there is an underlying story locked in your psyche. Uncovering the why will allow you to overcome the places you are stalled. Do the work, dig deep so that you can bloom.

Declaration: TODAY I will dig deeper to find out the reason I am stuck. I will find out because the most important thing I can do for myself is to become the person I want to be.

Rev. Dr. Tikeisha Harris

DAY 14

Change Your Perspective

THE WAY WE respond to life events is largely due to the perspective from which we experience them, which explains why two people can endure the same situation but will have very different perceptions of what occurred. If our perspective is negative, then our assumed outcome will also be negative. On the contrary, when your outlook is positive, it follows that the perceived outcome will also be positive. Our words have power, and there is power in positive thoughts.

Don't fret about using too many resources, rejoice in the availability of those resources to meet the need. In the same manner The Creator made provision before; He will make provision again. You can fret over the fact that you spent all your money paying bills, or rejoice because there was money available to pay the debt. The situation doesn't change, but your perspective has.

Two- dimensional holograms used to be a pop-culture hit in the 80s. Embedded in the same image are two or more pictures; however, you can only see one picture at a time. The picture you see depends solely on the way the light hits it. The paper doesn't change, but shining a different light will cause the picture (your perspective) to change.

<u>Declaration</u>: TODAY I will shine a new light on what I see.

Trgina Renae' Hunter

DAY 15

Freedom of Choice Given by God

RISE FROM THE murky water that has clouded your path to the destination of life. So many have said go this way or that. Yes, you can. No, you cannot. Just remember that God created you competent and capable of making your own choices. This freedom of choice was a gift from God for your eyes only. Do not let others open your presents and rob you of a defined path perfectly packaged for your life journey.

If you do not know who you are and where you are going, then ask God for those directions, and He will make your path clear.

Declaration: TODAY I choose to rest in peace by releasing all fear and uncertainty of my future endeavors and will seek God each day for direction in my minute-by-minute choices.

Dr. Sharon Foreman

DAY 16

Be Clear About Who You Are

WHEN NAVIGATING THROUGH life and trusting in life's process, knowing who you are is important. Being aware of your motives, desires, pain, and joy will allow you to experience evolution differently. You will evolve and grow in all facets of your life, which will allow you to build on your strengths and improve your weaknesses. You will no longer seek the approval of others; instead, the validation will come from within due to your heightened level of awareness.

<u>Declaration</u>: TODAY I will be intentional about the words I use to affirm myself, and I will dedicate time to self-care.

Tarnisha Esco

DAY 17

Who Am I?

WE OFTEN HEAR about having thirty seconds to give our elevator speech to sell someone on our product, business, or skills. Most people are good at promoting others, but not so well at promoting themselves. The reason it is difficult for many of us to promote ourselves is that we spend an enormous amount of time tending to others, and we do not have time to focus on ourselves. All too often, intertwined with our happiness is pleasing and appeasing others, and we don't know who we are or what we want. We put our needs on the back burner and become complacent as it relates to ourselves.

You must become fully immersed in defining who you are and what you desire. The day of settling and going along to get along is over. Today is the day you unlock your potential and create an abundance of love, joy, and peace within yourself.

Declaration: TODAY love, peace, and joy overflows within me! I create abundance and prosperity chases after me!

Dr. Salim Bilal-Edwards

DAY 18

It's Your Time

THE ALARM GOES off; you jump out of bed, a thousand and one thoughts running through your head. Cook breakfast, make lunches, lay clothes out, too; that's just the beginning, there is so much more to do. Drop-off, pick-up, get to work on time – there are still a hundred things running through your mind. Get the groceries, the toiletries, and everything on your list, double-checking in your head for something you may have missed.

You've checked all the boxes on your list of things-to-do, but there's one thing on your list you've neglected, and that's YOU!! You matter, you're important, and you deserve attention too. While doing all these things for everyone else, please don't forget you.

Take a minute to relax and quiet your mind, take a minute or two for you – It's your time!

Declaration: TODAY I will take a few minutes out of my busy day to focus only on ME!

Rev. Dawn W. Adams

DAY 19

Be Present

WHAT DOES IT mean to be present? It means to be focused, in-tuned, and aware of the present moment. Every moment you experience brings out a certain aspect of who you are. Who you were in the past- and yes, yesterday was the past- it does not necessarily dictate who you have to be today. You should know and acknowledge who you are but also who you aspire to be. Who do you want to be for yourself and others? What part of yourself do you want to share?

When you stay in the present moment, you can identify who and what you are. Then ask yourself, is this who I *really* am? If it is, keep at it. If it isn't, now you can identify the adjustments you may want to make.

Declaration: TODAY I will focus on being in every moment I experience so I can be and give the best of me to the world.

Candice Jackson

DAY 20

Know My Name

MOST PEOPLE DON'T want to know the truth about themselves. That's why we are so distracted by social media, food, and reality TV. Distraction is easier than facing the truth of what is going on in your life. But when you become self-aware, you can capitalize on your strengths and work around your weaknesses to create a life that truly satisfies you.

Self-awareness is available to all but only pursued by a select few. When you know yourself, it becomes easier to be successful. You can maneuver around your weaknesses. You can take full advantage of your strengths. You learn how to manage yourself and understand what makes you tick.

Declaration: TODAY I will be aware of what makes ME, and intentionally operate in my strengths while not allowing my weaknesses to consume me.

Gail Crowder

DAY 21

Self-Conscious Not Self Conscious

YOU ARE LEARNING to be comfortable in your own skin. It's new but refreshing to fearlessly show others who you are. Don't be conscious of shining your light, instead marvel at how bright your light shines.

Declaration: TODAY I am boldly walking to my destiny. I am aware of my "potential." Meaning I know great things are coming my way and I have the ability to rise to each and every occasion. On this journey of life, I have so much farther to go, I can do it and therefore I will do it. My light will shine brighter than ever before.

Angela Jewel Brown

DAY 22

I'm Real to Me!

Look at yourself in the mirror. Who do you see? I just see me, looking back at me.
Are you how they see you? Is it their reality? Are you blinded by the masks hiding in the
shade and darkness of stories untrue? Are you sure this is really you?
What's your identity? Be honest with yourself. For in truth, that's where you'll see.
When you are real with yourself. That's where you are free.

I am truth, love, and light. I know this about me. I've looked in the mirror, and now I
truly see I embrace my identity. Knowing who I am means being real. Knowing how
I am to deal, knowing what makes me feel. How I react, tick, and appeal. I have an
identity. I know in truth. I am real to me!

LOOK IN THE mirror. Undoubtedly, you see the perfection God created. Now, look beneath the surface and be honest about what you see (remember that this is not what others perceive of you but what you know and accept of self). "Who am I? What is my identity? What qualities do I possess, and what beliefs do I hold fast to?" These are some questions to ask yourself for a better understanding of who you are. Before you can be self-aware, you must accept your identity. Once you accept your identity, nurture, protect, and love your identity. Operate in the freedom and truth of who you are. If you are not true to yourself, how can you be true to others? Knowing oneself is loving oneself. How can you love who you don't know? Know thyself!

Declaration: TODAY I will operate in freedom and the truth of who I am, because I'm real to me!

Sandy Buchanan-Sumter

DAY 23

Free to Be You

Mini skirt, crop top, torn jeans, bobby socks

Long hair, short hair, purple hair – don't care

I have a husband you have a wife

You do you it's your life

Thrift store find or designer clothes

At the end of the day who really cares or knows

If you're looking for something you will definitely find it

But it's my business and my life so let me mind it

What's right for you, may not be right for me

But we can still co-exist and both be free!

Declaration: TODAY I will be intentional about freely being ME!

Rev. Dawn W. Adams

DAY 24

Unity Check~Who's on Your Team?

UNITY [YOO-NI-TEE], NOUN: 1. the state of being one; oneness. 2. Oneness of mind, feeling, etc., as among a number of persons; concord, harmony, or agreement.

How's your support system? When you need help, after prayer, who can assist you? Are the folks you surround yourself with good positive people? Do they support your dreams? If not, it's time for a unity check. Be careful; when discord arises, you should pause and treat it as a flashing caution sign. You may find yourself amongst dream killers and stealers. Don't get me wrong, not everyone will understand you or your dreams. Many may not believe in your aspirations, but you can't let that stop you. Just push past them, step away from the negative comments and naysayers, even if it's close family or friends. Still love them, but it may be that you cannot share the details of your dreams, especially if doing so clouds your thinking and adds self-doubt. You have innate abilities and strengths. Become an expert in what makes you soar. There are certain resources, conditions, and people that empower you. Know what they are and use them. Build a network of them and keep them close. Focus on the steps that will lead to success. What will it take? Who will it take? The bottom line is that it's your dream.

Declaration: TODAY I will do a "Unity Check" and unite only with supportive and positive people.

Yolanda 'Loni' Chinn

DAY 25

Shine Bright

IF YOU HAVE ever been assaulted, had a major illness, or experienced a substantial financial loss, then you have experienced trauma. That traumatic experience may have caused you to dim your light. Maybe you have been too afraid to show up to your life out of fear that everything would fall apart again. Perhaps, you just heard so many times that you are nothing that you started to think you weren't anything. Whatever your traumatic story has caused you to think about yourself or what you're capable of, this can be the day you break up with it.

It won't be easy, but it's time you stop letting your previous experiences dim your light. Instead, decide that you're turning up your light, and it will be a brilliant, blinding light at all costs. To do that, you might need to read self-help books or practice saying affirmations. Maybe you need to hire a life coach or go to therapy, or you might need to do all of these or a combination of them. But decide that you won't keep crying and beating up yourself. Decide you won't stay stuck anymore. Instead, go after the root cause and address the trauma you've faced in your life. It's time that you shine bright. Do whatever is necessary to discover what's holding you back and take the steps for your brilliance to impact the world.

<u>Declaration</u>: TODAY I refuse to let my trauma define me. I couldn't control the trauma, but I can control my response. I will do whatever it takes to make my light shine bright again.

Rev. Dr. Tikeisha Harris

DAY 26

Spring Cleaning

MANY OF US can fit the descriptions of extroverted-introverts or popular-loners. We function well in a room full of people, but at any given moment, we would much rather be alone. As we mature, we discover that we can enjoy our own company. Dinners, movies, the museum, the Kennedy Center...whatever, with no one to criticize our choices, talk through the movie, or complain about how they don't like the food at the restaurant chosen for the evening. The best perk: no haggling over who only ate the salad when the bill comes.

Introversion for some of us isn't a character trait; it becomes our choice. We must wisely choose who we will spend time in our spiritual, emotional, and intellectual spaces. Any negativity disrupts that space. Take inventory of how certain people upset your calm and began to move differently where they are concerned. Self-awareness requires introspection about who you are and for identifying who and what is important in your journey. My journey has taught me that there will come a time when you have to decide to protect your interpersonal space and the peace that affects your being. It will become necessary to put some distance between yourself and the negative people who occupy your space. Doing so will make room for new people who will share your intention to protect your peace simply because they know how to protect their own. Knowing yourself allows you to clean up your heart space and check your roster.

Declaration: TODAY I will make the necessary personnel changes to protect myself and my peace.

Trgina Renae Hunter

DAY 27

I AM

THE SIMPLE PHRASE I AM permeates the spirit and catapults us into living our best life. I am not who others say I am. I am not my past, for I grow daily. I am fearfully and wondrously made marvelous in God's sight. Made in the image of God, I am connected to God and to the power source that resides in me. I have divine authority to create a meaningful life free of drama and cares of this world. Being connected to my Power Source (God) I can speak life over dead situations as well as the ability to cast out negative things that try to arise in my daily walk. I am royalty and a ruler over all things in my sphere of influence. I am an overcomer and yes, more than a conqueror.

<u>Declaration</u>: TODAY I declare and decree that I will live my best life!

Dr. Salim Bilal-Edwards

DAY 28

Don't Be Afraid of Growth!

ARE YOU THERE? Have you ever been asked this question and your trying to figure out why? Yes, I have. As people often times we are showing up for others but never enough for ourselves. Have you ever searched for answers to your problems? The truth is the answer lies within you. What a great feeling! A person needs to be fully present and engaged in your journey of discovery to appreciate the process. When you are constantly running from self-awareness, you prolong your growth. Stop running in circles and become the key to your own success story.

The act of self-awareness requires you to be honest, true and fearless. Be willing to strive towards your best daily. Practice placing yourself first and get comfortable with being uncomfortable.

<u>Declaration</u>: TODAY I will acknowledge that I have grown from my past to embrace my future.

Nanyamka A. Payne

DAY 29

Going Through Changes

UNDERSTAND THAT CHANGE must happen in order for you to grow. Say it: I'm on my way to change and growth. Believe you can make the change. Which do you prefer? Bondage or Breakthrough? You must accept change and move on. Awareness is the key to growth. Face it, so you can fix it! What do you need to change to be a better You?

<u>Declaration</u>: TODAY I will accept the changes that come my way.

Yolanda 'Loni' Chinn

DAY 30

A Microscopic View

WISDOM INTO YOUR own life starts with awareness, consciousness, and the courage to put yourself under a microscope. You'll gain a microscopic view of all the small, unseen, yet intricate factors that have shaped you, along with your willingness to acknowledge and understand the true reasons behind what makes you tick.

Being self-aware is a form of healing that flows from the inside out and allows you to restore your mind, heart, and spirit, giving back your life, identity, and power.

Declaration: TODAY I will start the journey to getting to know myself, and start the healing of those broken pieces from the inside out.

Tawawn Lowe

Self-Esteem & Self-Confidence

"Our deepest fear is not that we are inadequate. Our deepest fear is that we are powerful beyond measure. It is our light, not our darkness that most frightens us. We ask ourselves, 'Who am I to be brilliant, gorgeous, talented, fabulous?' Actually, who are you not to be? You are a child of God. You playing small does not serve the world. There is nothing enlightened about shrinking so that other people won't feel insecure around you. We are all meant to shine, as children do. And as we let our own light shine, we unconsciously give other people permission to do the same. As we are liberated from our own fear, our presence automatically liberates others."

- Marianne Williamson

Self Esteem

A confidence and satisfaction in oneself.

Self-Confidence

A feeling of trust in one's abilities, qualities, and judgment.
A confidence in oneself and in one's powers and abilities.

Beloved,

This life is full of joy and pain, peaks and valleys, and experiences that shape your beliefs and thoughts about yourself. Your self-esteem and self-confidence are important to your journey. They are the pulse of your beliefs about yourself and your abilities, which can work for you, or against you achieving the happiness and success you desire.

Having healthy and positive self-esteem and self-confidence is imperative to your happiness and success. You have to be willing to believe in yourself, your strengths, talents, and ability to make a difference in your own life. Build your self-esteem on facts. Identify, practice, and focus on your strengths to help you build a solid and healthy foundation for your self-esteem. Build your self-confidence upon your belief in your competence and ability to succeed. The more success you experience, the more confidence you develop to believe in yourself.

Self-esteem and self-confidence can be just as fragile as an egg, and you have to be careful of how you, and others handle you. Don't allow people or yourself speak death into your life, or about your life. Learn from your disappointments and failures, but don't allow them to dictate who you become, or what you can achieve. You are in charge of you, and that means you are in charge of protecting and the well-being of your self-esteem and confidence.

Everybody Needs A Little TLC!

Your self-esteem and self-confidence are empowering factors. It is the TLC you need for healthy and positive feelings and thoughts to take action to achieve your best self and best life.

DAY 31

Be Your Own Cheerleader

STOP WAITING FOR other people to cheer you on, clap for you, or give you that pep talk you need.

It is nice when other people pump you up, but you don't need other people to always do what you can do for yourself. Believe enough in yourself to be your own cheerleader, and boost your own self-esteem and confidence. Use your self-talk to cheer yourself on. Don't be scared to tell yourself you are awesome, to pat yourself on the back, to give you that pep talk, or to say you did the **DAMN THING**!

Stand tall, say it yourself, and tell others, **I AM AWESOME**!

<u>Declaration</u>: TODAY I will be my number one cheerleader, always cheering for myself, patting myself on the back, celebrating and affirming myself, unapologetically.

Tawawn Lowe

DAY 32

The Only Opinion that Matters is Mine!

"**THE MOST IMPORTANT** opinion you have is the one you have of yourself, and the most significant things you say all day are those things you say to yourself."

Declaration: TODAY the only opinion about me that matter is mine. I take charge of the health of my self-esteem and confidence, and reject anything that speak against my truth.

Author Unknown

DAY 33

You Are Not Your Past

YOUR PAST IS just that- your past! It is not who you are, it does not dictate your future, and it is not a place for you to stay. You are more than your past; you are the extraordinary total of your life experiences. Everything you've gone through and everything you've experienced has made you the awesome human being you are today.

So know your truth, live your truth because there is no shame in owning every part of who you are. It's the truth that makes you free

Declaration: TODAY I will encourage myself to live in my present truth, and remember that I am not my past!

Rev. Dawn W. Adams

DAY 34

Live Life in Full Bloom

AS LONG AS the sun shines (this includes "liquid sunshine" a.k.a rain), you can choose joy, happiness, and peace. Understand who you are, whose you are, and where you'd like to go. Then Go!

Take Action. Don't get stuck, and yes, get out of your own way. Many times, we allow our fears and false beliefs to keep us in a space from which we need to move. We want to move; however, fear is the main culprit, like a paralysis, keeping us from moving. It becomes easier just to stay even when it's unbearable and or miserable. It's more comfortable to be amongst the known than the unknown no matter how dysfunctional that space can be. Inner peace is a necessity. It's an ingredient to being happy. Seek and find your inner peace. Set your mind for peace. Breathe! Move, learn, stretch yourself, and grow. Stop laughing at your dreams; find out how to make them your reality. Stop thinking of them as just silly ideas. Learn to live your dreams beyond just in your head. Write them down, speak them aloud, and then seek action plans. It's time to stretch and live beyond your comfort zone.

Dreams do come true if you wake up and live them!

Declaration: TODAY I will wake up my dream. I will live life in full bloom allowing my petals to blossom and thrive like grass in a field.

Yolanda 'Loni' Chinn

DAY 35

Who Pushed Me?

WHO PUSHED ME? Who shoved me? Who nudged me? God. God will continue to PUSH you until you come into an awareness of self. He will continue to challenge your very being, the fibers that he knitted together, the nerves that charge up your life, and the air that you breathe. Mediocracy is not an option when God is the head of your life. You have more than you need to succeed, you have what it takes, and you are the issue. You are in your own way waiting for confirmation, waiting for validation, waiting for a green light, when God said, "GO". The PUSH is what is required to make you move from that place of complacency. We tend to stand too long, stay too long, and sit too long while waiting on our miracle. You are the miracle.

From the time of conception, you were set to succeed, you were set to lead, and you were destined to finish the race. I dare you to swim as fast as you did that day, I dare you to walk as fast as did when you first learned to walk, I dare you to run as fast as you did when you first learn to run, I dare you to even crawl as fast as you did when you first learned to crawl. Self Esteem is born into us, and as we live our lives, the experiences diminish everything that built us.

Declaration: TODAY I will **rebuild.** I will take back my life. **I am not afraid.**

Sonya D. Webb

DAY 36

Be Whom You Choose to Be

SOMETIMES PEOPLE PUT labels on us because of what they think they see in us or hear about us. It's only their perception and not our reality. People may see the manifestation of experiences that have affected and changed our true character. People may also see what they want to see and look through their personal lens to make assumptions about who we are.

If we begin to believe what others think about us, we can lose our true identity. Don't be misguided by the opinions of others. Don't fall prey to the deception tactics of scorners or false accolades. It will take courage to stand in your space. It will take strength to be who you are and not the summation of your experiences. Let your journey be the pathway you walk and not the total creation of you. You can overcome bad experiences, and you can change behavior patterns. Think beyond any negative trials and tribulations you have encountered and center your thoughts on the greatness that you possess within. A walk down another pathway can be a change maker. Chose to walk in the direction you want to go, decide which path you want to follow, and let your true self emerge over the opinions of others.

<u>Declaration</u>: TODAY I am not who you think I am. I am not your perception. Today I am who I choose to be.

Rev. Sandra Williams

DAY 37

Redefine Normal

AT THE CORE of your existence is your natural instinct to survive. When life and livelihood are threatened, you either fight, flee, or adapt. When we feel powerless to fight or unable to flee, we often adapt. It's a coping mechanism. Somehow, we convince ourselves that it diminishes the resulting stress we experience. Adaptation allows you to find a way to accept that the spiritual, mental, emotional, or physical dysfunction is the best it's ever going to get, so you can justify the things that you have endured. After all, it is what it is, right? Wrong.

When you begin to rationalize this mental, spiritual, emotional bondage as normal, you validate it and make it normal. **IT. IS. NOT. NORMAL**. Your best life is a space of freedom and abundance like you've never seen!! Dream again. Place expectations on the promises of The Creator on YOUR life. PUT. IN. THE. WORK necessary to sustain once those promises manifest. The Bible says that faith without works is dead. It's no more than wishful thinking.

Many who are bound or trapped by their circumstances sometimes don't realize they are trapped until they become free. When training, baby circus elephants are bound on the ankle by a tether that they can not pull up. Once they grow to adulthood, they don't know they are strong enough to break away, because they stopped trying to pull away. You are stronger than you think. Pull up your tether and begin to dream a wonderful dream for your life. Believe in yourself, and what you can accomplish, **REDEFINE** your normal.

Declaration: TODAY I accept that I have the power to redefine what I call normal.

Trgina Renae' Hunter

DAY 38

Keep Your Head Up and Don't Let Your Crown Slip

KEEP YOUR HEAD up, and don't let your crown slip. You are a king or queen. Don't let anyone ever tell you differently. Your smile is brighter than the sun as it radiates the world. It doesn't matter what others say, let it roll off your back and keep your head up. Know and love who you are. Don't let others deter you from loving you and seeing your greatness. You are a king or queen whose crown sits pretty because greatness is within you.

Declaration: TODAY I see myself as the king or queen, I was created to be, loving myself, and the greatness within.

Angela Jewel Brown

DAY 39

Creating Self-Confidence

CONFIDENCE MAY NOT be an attribute that is innately inside of you, but you can develop it. You first must love yourself without judgment, even those parts of you that you don't like necessarily. Look at yourself with admiration, acceptance, and certainty. Think positive thoughts about yourself and speak them into existence to all who will listen – I am beautiful, strong, smart, loved, and God is always by my side. I will never give up on life, I will never lose hope, and I will always smile. As you walk in the glow of explicit optimism, you will feel your self-confidence and self-esteem strengthen. As you adopt a consistent, encouraging mantra that you affirm daily, your self-confidence will expand to all aspects of your life.

<u>Declaration</u>: TODAY I will create an attitude of positivity and allow only positive energy into my world – I am my own catalyst and will accept nothing short of greatness!

Dr. Rasheda Parks

DAY 40

You Are AMAZING

DO YOU REALIZE how AMAZING you truly are? God has created you with a purpose and a destiny. The world is waiting for you to come into a knowledge of who you are. Once you tap into the notion that you are fearfully and wonderfully made, NO ONE should be able to "tell you ANYTHING."

Start each day by affirming yourself while standing in front of a mirror. Your daily affirmations like, "I AM powerful," "I AM wonderful," "I AM amazing" and "I AM beautiful," will raise your self-esteem meter. You will go out each day with your head held high and your chest out because you have spoken life to yourself. It is a process, and at times you may not believe that you are that special, but the more you hear yourself speak these words to yourself, you will believe that you have purpose and that your impact on the world will be great.

Declaration: TODAY I accept and acknowledge that I am powerful, I am strong, I am impactful, I am intentional, and I am amazing! There is NOTHING I cannot do. My impact on the world is mighty, and I am grateful God has created me for this time.

Kim Reed-Butler

EVERYBODY NEEDS A LITTLE TLC

DAY 41

You Cannot Buy Confidence!

I AM STRONG! I am Confident! I am a Warrior! If you are looking to pick-up a bottle of confidence from your local pharmacy, please do not be disappointed when you do not find it. Your hard work, constant nurturing of your soul, prayer and daily affirmations is where it can be found. Place affirmations in the following places: Around the mirror in your bathroom, in the visor of your car, on your dresser, in your shoes, in your wallet, desk at work/home and closet doors.

The mind is very powerful! And promises to be a part of your self-confidence journey as you strut boldly to the beat of your own drum. Always remember that everyone has his or her own goals and dreams their fulfilling. Do not be intimidated by this. Just keep going.

Declaration: TODAY I accept that I am flawed with imperfections, but I am me.

Nanyamka A. Payne

DAY 42

You Inspire You

Muse - a person or personified force who is the source of inspiration for a creative artist (The Merriam-Webster Dictionary, 2019)

YOU ARE THE creative artist painting, sculpting, and molding the life you want. No one has the authority to tell you who you are or how important you are to this world. Many things can be an inspiration, people, nature, etc. BUT what if they aren't there? What if you feel your creativity is blocked? Who or What can help you get up and keep going when you are feeling down?

The answer is YOU. Before anyone sees the amazing person you are, you must see it first. Believe in yourself. Know that you can rely on and trust in yourself. Know that you can and will do.

When you walk out into the world, you are the personified force that is the source of your inspiration for greatness.

Declaration: TODAY I am my own muse. I inspire me. I can do everything I need to do today.

Candice Jackson

DAY 43

Who Will Paint Your Picture?

DON'T LET OTHER people paint your self-portrait with their creative constraints and limited abstract understanding of who they think you are. No one can paint you brighter than yourself. You are the artist of your life. You can decide how you want your portrait to appear. You get to choose the option of airbrush or paintbrush, and the color and hues you want to use to depict how your true beauty will be displayed.

Declaration: TODAY I am the creative artist of my life, and TODAY I will choose how my portrait will look.

Tawawn Lowe

DAY 44

I Am Who I Say I Am!

WHEN YOU BECOME clear about who you are, you'll exude love, respect, courage, confidence love for yourself. In order to honor and love yourself you have to first identify, accept, or change your flaws while celebrating your greatness.

<u>Declaration</u>: TODAY I will take time and reflect on me & fall in love with me.

Tarnisha Esco

DAY 45

Believe in Your Yes!

IF SOMEONE TOLD you "no," but your inner spirit was saying "yes," don't stop at no. Believe in yourself and your yes. Prepare for your yes, strive for your yes, and wait for your yes. Today you might receive a no, but expect to get your yes.

Life has its twists and turns, ups and downs, joyful moments, and sad times, but nothing should stop you or hold you back from getting to your "yes."

Life has a way of zapping your energy, dulling your enthusiasm, stripping away your creativity, and drowning your dreams. But today is the day to toss out the zappers, leap for joy, and let your creative juices flow into your hopes and dreams.

"No" is just a stepping-stone on the way to achieving your goals. With each step you take, you are increasing your belief that you can, and you will conquer the challenges that may come your way.

Yes, you are, yes, you can, and yes, it shall be.

Declaration: TODAY I will believe in me; my times are in God's hands and know my "yes" is on the way.

Rev. Sandra Williams

DAY 46

Take A Leap of Faith - JUMP!

"THE BEST WAY to gain self-confidence is to do what you are afraid to do."

Declaration: TODAY I will take a leap of faith and do something outside of my comfort zone, it will be no loss, but lessons learned, and I will find victory in doing it scared.

Author Unknown

DAY 47

When God Made You, He Truly Made Something Special
TM

SELF-ESTEEM IS INCREDIBLY important. I think it is so important that I am going to say that again. Self-esteem is incredibly important. Many people have the notion that it is the same as self-confidence; however, it is far more than just self-confidence. If we look further into the origins of the word esteem itself, as we look etymologically, it comes from the word an estimate, which means 'to put a value on.' As you might guess, this word shares the same root as 'estimate'. Therefore, we can see that self-esteem means the value we put on ourselves.

When you have high self-esteem, you have a genuine, deep-rooted sense of self; you like (and often love) yourself; you can and do recognize and are in control of your internal state, and you have a sound sense of purpose, or rather you act and behave with purpose.

Declaration: TODAY I will remember I am truly something special!

Gail Crowder

DAY 48

Lift Up Your Head with Poise

LIFT UP YOUR head with poise. Let the world see the best of you even when it is raining in the inside. Laugh when the rain comes. Jump up and down in the puddles of water and splash it on the ground. Tomorrow is a new day, and the weather will change. Therefore, keep your confidence in the Lord, and life will be marked with ease, coolness, and freedom of humiliation.

Holding your head down when things move in the wrong direction will decrease your belief in being great at what you do.

Declaration: TODAY I choose to be fearless and make choices and accomplishments that feed my passion for making me feel happy and proud of who I am by trusting God.

Dr. Sharon Foreman

DAY 49

Chosen

DO YOU KNOW what is so wonderful about discovering that you're chosen? You realize you are the missing link. You're the missing puzzle piece we have been waiting on you for this day and time, so walk into the unknown. Your moment, your time, the birth of your voice, your words, your art, your vision, your charisma and character, the way you love others, the way you care for others, the way you help heal others in need. Now your purpose has simmered like Gumbo in a big pot, and now it's time to be dipped out for the greater good because you are chosen. You are prepared to teach, help, give, and minister in a way only you can. You've got the scars, the war wounds, to prove it, and you're the choice for more than one event.

You are a warrior chosen to come in and bring order, correct things, and placed them in their proper places, because of how you march through valleys, how you travel through rough trenches, and how you had to fight to get what was rightfully yours. Because reaching and stepping out on faith is all you know how to do. If you're supposed to be on the front line, you're there. If you operate as a helper, you're the best helper they've ever had. Whether you are in the background, or on the sideline, you know how to shine. Wherever you are planted, your gift and purpose will manifest together because you were chosen to walk out your destiny.

Declaration: TODAY I choose to do a good work and carry it to completion, because I am chosen.

Tasha Graham

DAY 50

Yes, You Can!

YOU CAN, YOU must, and you definitely will. There is no limit to what you can do. You are boundless. You can do anything you set your mind to do. Anything. Remember always to trust yourself, your skills, and, most importantly, your ability to learn and grow. Don't sweat trying to convince other people what you are made of, and what you can or cannot, do. The only person that can keep you from your "Yes, You Can!" is you. Don't be your limitation. You deserve greatness, and you are worth what you want. Go and make things happen because you deserve it. Remember, yes, you can, you have to believe you can, and you will.

Declaration: TODAY I will approach life with the belief that I can do all things – there are no limits to what I can do.

Pamishia Boyd

DAY 51

That Thing Good!

WHENEVER I DO something that one of my friends thinks is good, they exclaim, "That Thing Good!" It makes me smile and encourages my spirit.

When you do something that you feel is good, even if no one else agrees, tell yourself, "That Thing Good!" When you finally accomplish that task that has been taking what seems like forever, tell yourself, "That Thing Good!"

It's not proper English, and it's not meant to be – it's meant to encourage and acknowledge the good in you.

Declaration: TODAY I will remind myself when I do or say something good, even if no one else recognizes or acknowledges it, "That Thing Good"!

Rev. Dawn W. Adams

DAY 52

Just A Vacancy

JUST A VACANCY- low self-esteem and lack of confidence don't live here anymore.

When you lived inside of me, you caused self-doubt, stole my confidence, I allow the emptiness and loneliness make me feel like I was not enough, unworthy, and didn't deserve the desires of my heart.

So, I have abandoned you and found a new place to call home.

Because I love and need me so, confidence, self-assurance, peace, and happiness are my new place called home.

Declaration: TODAY I will abandon low self-esteem, insecurities, and lack of confidence, because I love and need me.

Tawawn Lowe

DAY 53

Love Lifted Me

IN 1912 JAMES Rowe penned the song "Love Lifted Me." The song tells of how we drift off into our own space and place, leaving the confines of God's Grace to our demise. The song was written from a spiritual place, but let's look at the title from a personal perspective, or shall we say the indwelling of our soul.

Too often, we look to external entities for our source of happiness, peace, and joy, only to find ourselves in a hole of despair and repeating the cycle of looking for another external entity to pick us up and give us joy. As James Rowe wrote, it wasn't until God heard his cry was, he lifted to a place of safety and security. Likewise, it's not until we look into the depths of our soul and draw on the energy of LOVE OF SELF and FOR SELF will we find ultimate happiness, peace, and joy.

We need to allow the indwelling of self- love to lift us to a place in which we are completely whole.

Declaration: TODAY I will not yield to the temptation of looking at external forces for my happiness. I will look deep inside my soul and feast on the love that's welling up that will continuously propel me to everlasting Happiness, Peace, and Joy!

Dr. Salim Bilal-Edwards

DAY 54

Do-Overs

"**YOU BETTER CHECK** yourself, before you wreck yourself." is usually the response you provide to someone else, who has crossed the line- **Boom, Bang, POW**!! If you grew up in the 70s, you know you just got dealt with it!! But what if the person is you? How often do you apply that phrase to your own life? If we're honest, the answer is never. We all tend to check the pulse of the people around us but fail to keep ourselves in check. Introspection is the in-depth inspection of your very being, your soul, and your heart.

It takes a great deal of self-confidence and honesty to inspect yourself. But, when you begin to understand who you are, you will begin to understand how your experiences have shaped your life. First, nothing that has happened has been by coincidence. Your life has been planned since the day you were just a mere thought, and that is hard to conceive. What changes your path is your ability to choose. Let's face it; we have all made some questionable decisions that sometimes have us reaching for the "DO OVER" button.

Declaration: TODAY I will do **IT** over. TODAY I will make **IT** right. TODAY I'll do **IT**!

Sonya D. Webb

DAY 55

You Are Fabulous. Period

WHILE THERE ARE many books about how to live your best life, there's no step-by-step book on making the absolute best decisions for your own life. We make the best decisions we can with the variable facing us at that time. You had no predecessor, and no precedent set as to how you can be your best you. No one has ever been YOU; neither did they have your exact variables. Attempts to dictate the quality of your life and decisions come from a second- hand, or third-hand perspective, AT BEST.

The only standard that exists for you and the only person you have to compete with or compare yourself to is who you were yesterday. If you can be a better you today than you were on yesterday by using the knowledge you've gained, what more can you do? Be you, unapologetically, because anyone trying to dictate what's best for you has never lived YOUR life.

Life really is what you make it. Most of us endeavor to make it the best we can, using the resources available to us. You don't have to have celebrity status resources to be completely fulfilled. You only need to realize how fabulous you are. Change your mindset and perspective. It can be that simple. No one on this earth can beat you at being you. You are doing an ABSOLUTELY FANTABULOUS JOB at being you!

Declaration: TODAY I embrace my FABULOSITY and the fact that I don't need anyone other than me to be **Fabulously Me**.

Trgina Renae' Hunter

DAY 56

I'm Good, and I Know It!

WE ARE ALL born with talents, gifts, and special skills specific to us. There are things that you do better than most people. What are those things? Don't doubt yourself and your abilities. Don't be critical of yourself. Affirm those things about yourself that are good and do things to build you up! Focus on accomplishments instead of failures. Treat yourself to something – a new hairstyle, delectable chocolate, a spa appointment, a day of rest, a long bubble bath, a pair of earrings. Do something nice for someone who needs help (taking the focus off self and assisting someone in need will boost your confidence!). So, what other ways can you affirm your AWESOMENESS? It starts in the mind. If you believe it, all things are possible.

Declaration: TODAY I am equipped with special talents, gifts, knowledge, and abilities, and I know that I'm good at what I do. I trust me, and I am confident!

Sandy Buchanan-Sumter

DAY 57

Being Confident is NOT Synonymous with Arrogant

- Confidence - a feeling of self-assurance arising from one's appreciation of one's own abilities or qualities (The Merriam-Webster Dictionary, 2019)
- Arrogance - having or revealing an exaggerated sense of one's own importance or abilities (The Merriam-Webster Dictionary, 2019)

Has anyone ever told you that you are arrogant when you've congratulated yourself? This happens because people don't know the difference between healthy confidence and arrogance. Being confident means that you are aware of your talents and value. It does not mean you aren't aware of your weaknesses. Just that you aren't focused on those right now.

In arrogance, you base your assessment on just the successes. You fake it until you make it. You hide failures and weaknesses. You must be better than everyone else. In confidence, you base your assessment on your total experience: both successes and failures. You give your best, and you know if someone gave a bit better, it does not diminish your talents and value.

Declaration: TODAY I am confident whether I win or misstep, and I will show it to the world freely.

Candice Jackson

DAY 58

The Authentic Me!

THE LATE POP Icon Michael Jackson sang about the man in the mirror. The first line says, "I'm gonna make a change for once in my life. It's gonna feel real good; gonna make a difference. Gonna make it right." The reality is that life has thrown many of us curveballs, and we have become comfortable living in our mess. When looking in the mirror, we only see our failures and mistakes, but that's a frosted image of our authentic self. We have been looking in the circus mirror, giving us a distorted image, and we have accepted that image to be how we really look.

To make a sincere change in how we think and feel about ourselves, we must change the narrative of how we currently view ourselves. TODAY get from in front of the distorted circus mirror and look at yourself through the mirror of gratitude. Look at yourself through the mirror of being an overcomer. Look in the mirror and see your authentic self.

Declaration: TODAY as I look in the mirror, I will see my life full of hope and possibilities for the future! I will see my authentic self. I will see a WINNER!

Dr. Salim Bilal-Edwards

DAY 59

I Can Do, I Can Do, I Can Do ALL Things!

THE FIRST STEP is trusting and believing that you can and then develop a plan of action. This plan will outline the steps you need to take, the places you need to go, the resources you need to grow, and the people you need to know. This plan will require a supernatural type of self-confidence. A confidence that will not take no for an answer, a confidence that will make you stand up, speak up, sit up, and get up! God has equipped you to do the ALL Things. You must decipher the thing that you are compassionate about, and you must ask God to begin to show you the plan for your life and to make it plain. Howbeit, you may have been chasing the wrong thing, and now you're wondering why it hasn't prospered. The thing is that thing was not part of God's plan. You ran out of strength.

You seemed to have missed the part about doing all things through Christ who will strengthen you. Knowing that you have a God-given strength to succeed will make you flex your muscles a little bit bigger, that strength will have you walking and talking with confidence. That God-given strength that's inside, you will begin to shift your narrative. Your journey will take you places you've never thought or imagined you'd be. Self-confidence requires a different set of eyes because you will begin to see in yourself what God already saw.

Declaration: TODAY I am that thing, and I am part of God's plan.

Sonya D. Webb

DAY 60

Giving Up Is Not an Option

WALK IN YOUR purpose boldly, even when defeat drifts your way. Desire, Focus and Vision all help you move in the right direction. Whatever it is ~ do it with Enthusiasm! It's ok to fall down and skin your knees. The important part is that you get back up and keep going. Learning from falls and failures are key ingredients to achievement. Sometimes you may need to shift directions. Know that you can do it! You can win!

<u>Declaration</u>: TODAY I will not give up! Giving up is not an option for me.

Yolanda 'Loni' Chinn

DAY 61

You Did It!

"**EACH TIME YOU** face your fears, you gain the strength, courage, and confidence you need to move forward, to bounce back, to start over, and to say you did it.

<u>Declaration</u>: TODAY I will just do it!

Tawawn Lowe

Self-Worth

"You alone are enough. You have nothing to prove to anybody".

– Maya Angelo

Self-Worth

The opinion you have about yourself and the value you place on yourself.

To have a favorable opinion or estimate of yourself. It means having unshakable faith in yourself and in your ability to follow through and get things done.

Beloved,

The moment God gave you this gift called life, you became valuable and necessary to this world; and the plans and purpose He has for your life. Your value and worth are internal and are based on the measure you set for yourself. Your value is not determined by your appearance, net worth, social status, what you do, nor what you achieve, but it's how you value yourself as a person.

You are valued and worthy even in your imperfection?

Your value is not in how other people see you, and it's not your job to make people see what you know. A lack of self-worth strips away your power. Don't give away your power waiting for approval outside of yourself, and stop undervaluing yourself because your life doesn't look like others. You alone determine your worth. It comes from being self-aware, accepting and understanding who you are, being confident in yourself; and knowing that your life has purpose, you are gifted, and all that mix with your life experiences makes you worthy.

Everybody Needs A Little TLC!

Self-worth is about knowing your worth. It is the TLC you need to accept your feelings of worthiness.

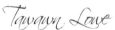

DAY 62

Stamp Yourself Approved!

YOU DON'T NEED anyone telling you who you are. Validation of who you are must come from within. Looking for validation outside of yourself is a set-up for disappointment. What you believe about yourself, who you can become, what you can achieve, and your self-worth is the only opinion that matters.

Waiting for other people to validate your worth and build you up diminishes your power to believe, love, and honor yourself.

Declaration: TODAY I choose to stop waiting for other people to validate me – I have the power to stamp myself **APPROVED.**

Tawawn Lowe

DAY 63

Know Your Worth in This Life

YOU ARE HERE for one important reason – TO LIVE YOUR BEST LIFE! You must live it abundantly, without regret and unapologetically. Never, ever compromise your integrity, morals, values, or dreams for anyone. Knowing how valuable you are is the key to establishing your self-worth with others. The most freeing feeling in this world is releasing your true self and not worrying or caring about acceptance.

Knowing your self-worth above how others may try to devalue you will establish respect and solidify your position as leader.

Declaration: TODAY I will assert myself as a leader by refusing to negotiate on the morals and values that have made me who I am. I am worthy of love and respect – nothing less.

Dr. Rasheda Parks

DAY 64

The Path of Your Destiny

BEYOND THE ROADS of life, there lies the path of your destiny. In that path are the roadblock intentions to make you stumble. In that path is the roadblock of decisions to make you grow. In that path is the roadblock of voices to steer you back and forth. Stop in your path and look at the stumbles. Stop to find that growth. Stop to filter through those voices. Stop to find the way God chose just for you.

Remember, God's ways are not our ways. He has chosen a path designed just for you, a foreordained destiny. I encourage you to take control of your future. Ask God for directions and wait for him to lead you in the right direction. Sometimes, it seems that He does not hear you. If you wait on God, even if it appears to be too long, you will see the benefits of those roadblocks intended to make you stumble. The decisions to make you grow will be clear and stable. Thus, the cycle repeats itself in the shaping of your destiny.

When you seek God for direction, He shows up on time. His timing is not the same as our timing. To understand this, you must wait on Him, expecting your resolutions, your growth, your breakthroughs. If you keep your focus on Him and do not lose hope, He will give you far above anything you could imagine.

<u>Declaration</u>: TODAY I chose to trust God as the creator of my destiny and will seek and wait on Him to direct my path.

Dr. Sharon Foreman

DAY 65

You Got This!!

YOUR VALUE DOES not come from others; you will ALWAYS be more than enough! Too often, we compare ourselves to others, thinking that we are less than them. Maybe you have heard negative words growing up from people, frequently as close as our family members, and have believed or accepted what they have said as the "truth." But what you MUST do is turn those words around and recognize you are VALUABLE.

You have what the world needs. Step into your greatness and fully embrace your unique self.

<u>Declaration</u>: TODAY I will accept that my self-worth comes from within. I am a valuable person created with a PURPOSE, ON PURPOSE, FOR A PURPOSE! I know I bring value to every endeavor. I am more than **ENOUGH!**

Kim Reed-Butler

DAY 66

You're Worth It

YOU ARE WORTHY of all the blessings that come your way. You are worthy of all the joy that comes into your life. You are worthy of all the love that you receive. Know your worth, and don't settle for less. No one can take away your worth unless you give them the power. The power within you cannot be diminished. Don't change yourself to make other people comfortable. You add flavor to the world that no one else can contribute.

Declaration: TODAY I know my worth. I am enough. I am worthy. What others say about me or to me doesn't diminish who I am. I will not change myself to make others feel comfortable because I am who I am. I deserve the world, and I will give it to myself.

Angela Jewel Brown

DAY 67

From Bondage to True Freedom

TRUE FREEDOM COMES when you commit to loving yourself so much that you understand your true value. Release yourself from self-doubt and the mask you wear that prevents the world from knowing who you are. You don't have to be who they want you to be instead become who you are destined to be. To do that, you have to be intentional and purposeful in your journey to becoming free. Trying to be who and what others want you to be is an attack on yourself. Release the burdens of the past and remember that you are worthy, and you are good enough.

Declaration: TODAY I know my past does not define my future; therefore, I'm releasing myself from all mental, physical, and emotional bondage.

Tarnisha Esco

DAY 68

Can You See Your Worth?

THE MIRROR IS only a reflection of what's on the outside. But your heart reflects who you are on the inside. No matter how much time you spend in the mirror perfecting your look, people will begin to see who you are by how you treat other people. That is your identity. The things you learned as a child ultimately shape your life. Your first lessons in life are learned in your household. You learn how to reason, how to count (money), how to lie, how to negotiate, what to eat, etc. Let's be real; you emulate what you see. Parents often say, "Do as I say, not as I do." But the truth is, a child will duplicate what they see you do. No matter the consequences, if you did it, they will do it too.

As adults, you can no longer hold on to "my parents did it that way; therefore, I'm the way I am." Adulating means you have a choice in choosing the narrative you want to live. You have the power to change the story, to turn the pages, and to perfect the outcome. Your path, your truth, and your journey don't have to align with anyone else's. I guarantee when you look in the mirror, you will see your reflection.

<u>Declaration</u>: TODAY I will affirm my place in this space, stating **I AM Worthy**.

Sonya Webb

DAY 69

You Are Worthy!

YOU ARE BORN worthy because God created you worthy. You don't have to earn it or achieve it. Just believe it. You are not someone else's definition of worth. You are not the description in the magazines or on a model's resume. Your value cannot be measured by a degree, a title, or a position. Your worth is unquantifiable and indescribable. You are worth the time, energy, and importance that you have placed on others. You deserve the best because you are the best. You are Worthy.

Failures don't define you. Mistakes don't disqualify you. Achievements don't earn your worth, and accomplishments don't validate you as an individual. You are already worthy. You are the essence of God's fabric woven into YOU, labeled "BEAUTIFUL and WORTHY."

<u>Declaration</u>: TODAY I accept that "I AM WORTHY, I AM Beautiful and Wonderfully Made." I AM, who God says I AM. "I AM WORTHY!"

Rev. Sandra Williams

DAY 70

Unapologetically You!

SO WHAT YOU are:

Amazing and Beautiful
Confident and Demanding
Encouraging and Fierce
Grateful and Humble
Intelligent and Joyful
Kind and Loving
Marvelous and Nifty
Optimistic and Passionate
Quintessential and Respectful
Sexy and Tenacious
Unique and Virtuous
Wise and Extra-ordinary
Young at heart and Zealous

You don't need permission to be who you are, so be unapologetically you!

Declaration: Remind yourself today how great you are from A-Z

Rev. Dawn W. Adams

DAY 71

See Yourself Through New Eyes

HOW VALUABLE AM I? **Am I worthy? Do I deserve what I want?** Have you ever said this to yourself? Most everyone thinks these thoughts in the back of their mind when something doesn't go the way they want. No matter how great life is to you, there will be times when you are faced with disappointments. When those disappointments come, you will dissect everything you did and everything you are. When you do, keep it healthy. How? Accept yourself if you did something you shouldn't have. Keep loving yourself if you messed up. Adjust yourself if you know new information that you didn't before. Dissect it but don't live in it. When you jump back up, see yourself through new eyes.

Your new eyes are fresh. They now know which way to look when you jump back into life. Your new eyes never saw defeat. They only see a trial to do again. Your new eyes see you're valuable and worthy to have what you want and will see that you get it.

Declaration: TODAY I am not defeated. I will use fresh eyes to evaluate this situation and keep pressing toward my goal

Candice Jackson

DAY 72

You're Worth It

MANY OF US enter into friendships, romantic relationships, and jobs giving the best parts of ourselves to keep others happy. We leave our dreams behind to support our spouse's goals, to meet bottom lines at work, and to be present for children. Even in friendships, we can spend most of our time listening to friends complain about their lives, when we know that we have a laundry list of things we want to do for ourselves. If you have found yourself in that position – the one where everyone else matters, and you subtly keep putting yourself off, make today the day you stop, If you need someone to validate you, your goals, your ability to just no, let this serve as the validation you've been looking for.

Nap, journal, start your yoga practice, type a few sentences on the laptop that will be the start to your first book. Stop living for everyone else and not for yourself because you're worth it!

<u>Declaration</u>: TODAY I will create space for me. I will not put myself on hold so that others can be validated. I accept that I am worth my own time.

Rev. Dr. Tikeisha Harris

DAY 73

Moving Forward

RELATIONSHIPS WITH PEOPLE should not ever make you feel like you're a nobody. Any time you're in a relationship with individuals, it should build you up as a person and not reduce you. So, every once in a while, you have to revisit God to be reassured that you're moving forward. And when you get that validation from God, that's the only validation you need in your life for your journey.

You can't back up in life because people don't like who you are, your confidence, your swag, your happiness, and joy. Keep moving forward. Tell them to talk to God; He made you. You don't have to take a backseat because of others' foolish behavior or act out of an urge to do wrong. You don't have to speak negatively about their life because they speak negative things about you to make themselves feel good. You don't even have to retaliate; you've got this, you know your worth! Because you know your worth, you don't have to get ugly because others don't know theirs. Because you are secure in who you are, you can take them by the hand and help them see their worth. There is room at the top for all of us.

Declaration: TODAY I take the stand to move forward because I know my worth!

Tasha Graham

DAY 74

You Were Born to Be Great!

YOU WERE CREATED and formed by God for greatness. Before you were born, God had a plan for you. Walk in your greatness. Trials and tribulations come to make us strong, know that whatever life throws at you that you are more than a conqueror. You must acknowledge your greatness. We often look at our circumstances and believe we are what people say we are or that we are our circumstances.

Diamonds and graphite have the same chemical composition, but one is more valuable than the other. Diamonds are hard, and graphite is soft and easy to break. Diamonds are formed through years of intense pressure. You are formed through tough times and tough situations. The tough times you may face only exist to solidify your greatness.

Declaration: TODAY I will tap into and feel the greatness within myself. I am a diamond with great value and not graphite, which crumbles at the slightest touch.

Dr. Salim Bilal-Edwards

DAY 75

TODAY I Choose ME

TODAY I MAKE myself a top priority. I take care of my needs first, and that helps me to be able to take care of the needs of others. I am an important person with important things to do. I deserve to be treated well by everyone, and that includes me. I treat myself well because I deserve it. I love myself.

I am as important as anyone else in the world. I demand that I treat myself accordingly.

Declaration: TODAY I choose to put an oxygen mask on my face before I assist others.

Gail Crowder

DAY 76

They Can't Put A Price on You

DON'T TELL YOURSELF you're worth it because you think it's "right", tell yourself you're worth it because you know and believe you're worth it. People may say you're a "dime piece" but believe it or not, you're invaluable. No one can ever put a price on you because you're more valuable than anyone can even comprehend.

<u>Declaration</u>: TODAY I accept that I don't need validation from anyone, especially those who don't understand where I've been, where I am, and where I'm going. My self-worth can't be gauged, only I could determine how much I am truly worth and even then, I am worth more than I can even grasp.

Angela Jewel Brown

DAY 77

See Your Worth Through Your Own Lens

KNOWING YOUR WORTH starts with thinking you are worthy. Never allow yourself to be defined by other people beliefs, see yourself through your own lenses. The lenses that shows you no matter what, you are special, you can achieve anything, and you deserve nothing but the best. The only person who need to accept you, is you.

<u>Declaration</u>: TODAY, I will only surround myself with those who value me, and see my worth.

Tawawn Lowe

DAY 78

Walk in Victory

WE HAVE SO many uplifting scriptures, inspirational songs, encouraging mantras, and enlightening phrases to help us understand who we are and strengthen our belief in ourselves. Yet with all of these powerful tools, a thought of deception manages to creep into our minds and causes us to doubt ourselves, to question our worth, and tear down our self-confidence. These thoughts come clothed in life's circumstances and bad experiences. Negativity and adversities manipulate us and torture us with unbelief. Lack of self-worth may cause you to think you have lost your royal status of living and loving the skin that you are in and the power of love you possess.

Today let's walk in victory. Let's proclaim your knowledge and truth. Let's stand on the word of God today. Let's sing and dance to the inspirational sounds of love and happiness. Let's encourage your hearts with joy and laughter. Today you will embrace the beautiful things in life, declare love for yourselves, and tell yourselves you are worthy. Know this, claim this, and walk boldly in your victory.

<u>Declaration</u>: TODAY I will walk in VICTORY!

Rev. Sandra Williams

DAY 79

Well, I Am, Who I Am!!

"WELL, I AM, who I am," is usually a rhetorical response and not an affirmation. The phrase, "I am who I am," is followed with, "People have me messed up." I beg to differ. It's not other people who have you "messed up." It's you. It points back to who you proclaim that you are. Negative cogitations follow the "I am" because that is what you present to the world. These definitions of self-infliction ultimately become part of your narrative. I'm always amazed at the words we attach to ourselves, "I am that Bitch." and then wonder why people treat you in that manner. Or "I'm not the one." The one for what?

Anything that you attach to yourself can be unattached, including negative people who are quick to attach their negative thoughts on you. Every day, challenge yourself to affirm who you are or who you would like to become and work towards meeting that goal. Self-actuation begins with recognizing that there are some things that you can work on to improve and rewrite your narrative. Who you were yesterday, is not who you are today. I dare you to start by practicing self-love, self-respect, and self- awareness. **Who do you believe that you are?** I AM ——————————— .

Declaration: TODAY I will begin the *inside* work and rewrite my story.

Sonya D. Webb

DAY 80

Pursuit of Love

FROM THE WOMB of the mother where life begins, so begins the pursuit of love. As a baby sucks from its mother's breast, love inhabits the heart. However, emotions connect to the heart and mind, and when intertwined with the world, it establishes new moods and personalities. It shapes how you value life and your pursuit of love. We must learn to release the emotions of neediness, detachment, and distress and ask God to replace them with abundance, inclusion, and contentment.

The key to living a life of extraordinary possibilities is to increase your relationship with God. I encourage you to see each day as a flowing stream of water that washes away your steps of yesterday. That leaves you needy of direction for today. Your pursuit of love will shift from feelings of neediness, detachment, and distress to become like a branch on a tree, nourished continually by God- full of abundance, inclusion, and contentment.

<u>Declaration</u>: TODAY I choose to call out those emotions affecting my heart and mind that is holding me back from receiving those extraordinary possibilities by seeking God daily in my pursuit of love.

Dr. Sharon Foreman

DAY 81

It's My Choice, and I'm All That!

IF YOU HAVE yet to realize how FANTABULOUS you are, today is a new day to make some new choices. You have free will to believe, speak, and think what you want! So, let's think differently! What you put into the atmosphere comes back to you, so if you focus on the negative, what will you get back? Negativity! If you focus on the positive, you get back positivity. Consider making a choice to believe, speak, think, and bring about those things wonderful, positive, and good. You are all that and a bag of chips, and much, much more!

Put that in the atmosphere! If you remind yourself, "I am great!" then you walk in that greatness.

Declaration: TODAY I acknowledge I am worthy, and I choose to be positive and speak life to myself! I'm all that!

Sandy Buchanan-Sumter

DAY 82

I Can Show You Better Than I Can Tell You

LOVE YOURSELF, SO others love you. Believe in yourself, so others believe in you. Respect yourself, so others respect you. You can show them better than you can tell them. When you know your worth, the way you treat yourself will set the standard for how others treat you.

<u>Declaration</u>: TODAY I will teach people how to treat me by how I treat and carry myself.

Tawawn Lowe

DAY 83

You Are Enough

THERE IS ENOUGH of you and in you for the journey ahead of you. You possess everything you need to make it through and to the next level of your journey.

Every time you show up, you are letting the universe know that you are prepared for all that it has to offer.

You are equipped not only for understanding, growth, and higher heights but also for deeper depths – you are **ENOUGH**!

<u>Declaration</u>: Every time you look in the mirror TODAY say – I <u>(insert your Name)</u> am more than enough!

Rev. Dawn W. Adams

DAY 84

Hey, Good Looking!

FEELING GOOD ABOUT yourself should be a holistic experience; from the inside out, which means you work on your spirit, mind, AND your body. You are not amazing just because of how you look on the outside, but it is a part of that triangle. Having a healthy body image is just as important as your spirit and character.

Someone can tell you that you are pretty or handsome. Someone else can tell you that you aren't attractive at all. When you look in the mirror, the only opinion that matters is YOURS. If you think you have work to do, then do it. BUT you are still amazing while you're going through that process. No matter your size, shape, or style, you are still attractive. Feel free to change your weight, change your style, and change your hair...just remember, you are still good looking.

<u>Declaration</u>: TODAY every time I see my reflection, I will look right into my eyes, give myself a smirk, and say, "Hey, Good Looking!"

Candice Jackson

DAY 85

I Look and Feel Great!

WE LIVE IN a society where our worth is valued at the dollar amount spent to look a certain way. As you grow so should your outlook on life, the view of success and image of self-worth. When you think of your worth place it at the top of your life. Do not allow past moments of self-doubt to over cloud your current view. Dress up every day, smile, do a victory lap and wave to the people. You look great!

I encourage you to speak life into yourself and imagine where you see yourself in 5 weeks, 5 months or even 5 years from now. Now run with my image, do not look back. Be committed to creating a life you deserve. You are valued at priceless. Stop comparing yourself to others; you are a matchless wonder!

Declaration: I no longer will discredit my worth; I'm valuable and precious.

Nanyamka A. Payne

DAY 86

See Yourself as Worthy

Life will cause you to question your worth and what you truly deserve. Refuse to believe anything other than you are worthy.

You are worthy of happiness,
You are worthy of peace,
You are worthy of love,
You are worthy of success,
You are worthy of prosperity,
You are worthy of abundance

YOU ARE WORTHY of everything, and all the goodness life has waiting with your name on it.

Declaration: Today I see myself as worthy of all the goodness life has to offer.

Tawawn Lowe

DAY 87

Priceless

YOU ARE PRICELESS! There is no price tag on your self-worth.

<u>Declaration</u>: TODAY I declare and decree that I am priceless, and my self-worth is non-negotiable.

Pamishia Boyd

DAY 88

There is Power in Self Forgiveness

YOUR WHOLENESS BEGINS when you find the strength to release yourself from the harm you caused yourself. There is power in forgiveness, and there will be times in your journey when you will have to forgive yourself.

There is power in your words, and your future self needs to hear you are sorry so that it can heal and reclaim itself, self-esteem and confidence.

Your future self is waiting to hear,

I AM SO SORRY I HAVE NEVER LOVED YOU ADEQUATELY ENOUGH.

I AM SORRY I NEVER PUT YOU FIRST.

I AM SORRY I DIDN'T LISTEN TO YOU.

I AM SORRY THAT I GAVE UP ON US.

I AM SORRY THAT I DIDN'T KNOW WHAT TO DO WITH THE PAIN.

I AM SORRY THAT I GAVE UP ON US.

I AM SORRY THAT I GAVE AWAY OUR WORTH.

I apologize. I now understand that we are loved, valuable, and God created us on purpose. We are worth fighting for. We are worthy of a second chance.

Will you forgive me?

Declaration: TODAY I will apologize to myself for the things I have done to myself, but most importantly, I will forgive myself, because I worth it.

Morgan Chapman

DAY 89

Beauty for Ashes

BEAUTY FOR ASHES Perhaps the statement, "Freedom is not free" is familiar. It truly isn't. Freedom of all sorts cost immensely. The sacrifices, pains and struggles are all real. They are the backbone of the freedom we strive to obtain. The "freedom" is just that much sweeter when you get it after the sacrifices, pain and struggles. You may not have created the problem but it's yours to heal. Heal it! Set yourself free from the guilt. You didn't create the pattern, but you can break it. Learn how. Give yourself permission to sit in the heartbreak, the disappointments so that you can heal. The past is over~ it can touch you not.

The question is are you over it? Are you going to leave behind the past? Aren't you ready? Oh, the prices we pay from not believing we're enough. We want to be chosen, not realizing we can choose ourselves. You don't have to live in the pain. Yes, you deal with it, but you don't have to live there. I'll take my Beauty any day, Bye Ashes! I earned it.

<u>Declaration</u>: TODAY I choose me. I choose Beauty!

Yolanda 'Loni' Chinn

DAY 90

The Thorny Truth

GOD WAS INTENTIONAL when He shaped you into one of His beautiful masterpieces. To protect your worth, He created your life to have thorns and prickly things – and He purposed them to protect and nurture your growth.

You are like a rose, and the thorns don't take away from your beauty, purpose, or worth.

Declaration: TODAY I will embrace my thorns, recognize them as a part of my beauty and growth, allow them to protect me, as they increase my worth.

Tawawn Lowe

About the Visionary of Everybody Needs A Little TLC

TAWAWN IS THE CEO of TLConsultancy, LLC, founder of the Women Walking in their Own Shoes™ Movement, an **Amazon #1 bestselling author**, certified life coach, speaker, and creator of *the Achieve Big Now Academy*™.

TLConsultancy is a woman-and minority-owned multifaceted company based in Maryland that provides consulting and mentorship to individuals; learning/leadership-based solutions for organizations, and the umbrella for the Women Walking in Their Own Shoes™ Movement. Tawawn has blended her formal education, various certifications, and over 25+ years of professional experience to assist **organization with leadership development; and individuals with maximizing their full potential to achieve success.**

Tawawn's Why... For more than half her life, Tawawn believed her life had no real purpose. She turned someone else's limited belief about her potential into a self-fulfilling prophecy, making it true. She secretly lived an unhappy and unfilled life because she believed success could not be a part of her story. After having an "aha moment", she realized she had given away her power. This revelation led to her taking full charge of her own destiny, and to envision a different future for her life.

In October 2012, TLE expanded their mission and launched the Movement - Women *Walking in their Own Shoes* (WWITOS) ™. The Movement is a clarion call to action to women globally to say, "YES", giving themselves permission to become their best selves, create their best lives, and achieve success on their own terms (walk in their own shoes).

TLC Publishing Company is her newest endeavor. Tawawn is using her publishing company as a platform to allow individual's voices to be heard through their words; and using non-traditional publishing to get their story, poems, and message to the masses.

Tawawn is here to serve you. Her goal is simple, to help others take charge of their destiny, transform visions into results, and achieve success on their own terms.

For additional information on TLC Publishing Company or TLConsultancy, please visit Tawawn on the web at

www.tawawn.com

WE WANT TO HEAR FROM YOU!

Go to www.tawawn.com/testimonials and leave a few comments about how this book has helped you with taking a closer look at yourself, becoming more self-aware, boost your self-esteem, confidence and self-worth.

Follow Us on Social Media

🐦 TL_Consultancy
📷 TL_Consultancy
🔲 Tawawn

EVERYBODY NEEDS
A LITTLE

T **L** **C**

TRANSFORMATIONAL   LIFESTYLE   CONTENT

90 DAYS

OF SELF-CARE AND SELF-LOVE
(MIND, BODY & SPIRIT)

PRESENTED BY

TAWAWN LOWE

EVERYBODY NEEDS
A LITTLE

T L C

TRANSFORMATIONAL   LIFESTYLE   CONTENT

90 DAYS

OF DREAMS, GOALS, AND INTENTIONAL LIVING

PRESENTED BY
TAWAWN LOWE